Little Life Lesson Books

Every Body's Different

A Children's Book
about Understanding that Everyone is
Unique and Special

Written and Illustrated
By Karri Andersen

This book is dedicated to Everybody that is different and to the People who love and take care of them.

"When you do things for others, not expecting to be paid,

You will be blessed, with things that can't be bought."

Karri Andersen

Every body's different.
   No body is the same.

Our faces look different
and we all have a
special name.

Some bodies need special
things to help them heal
or work better.

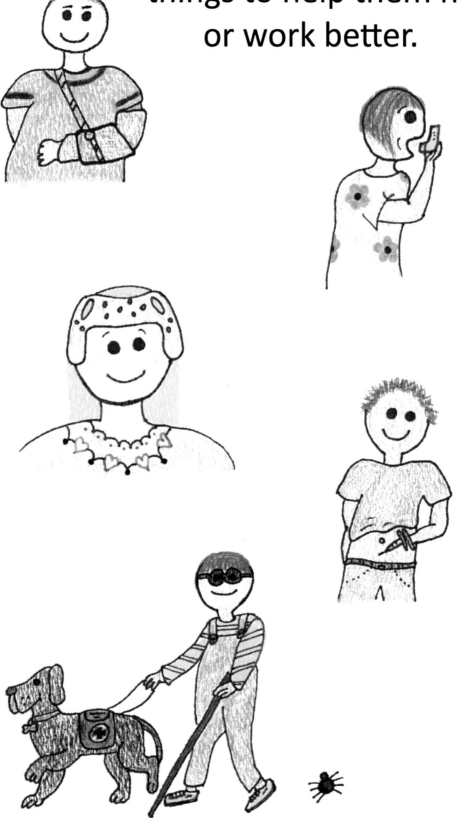

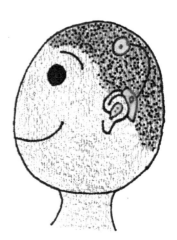

Like if Janet didn't have her glasses,

she couldn't read her letter.

Some nifty things might be
hidden inside bodies
or under clothes.

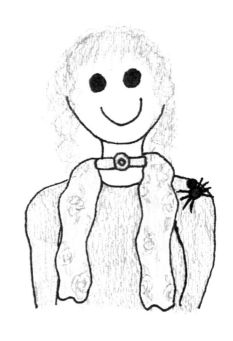

Others are not as
obvious, like someone
who needs to cover
their nose.

You may not
even notice
that these things
are there.

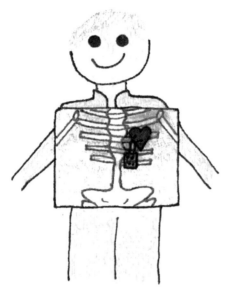

But they are very
important to help
bodies take
good care.

Lots of bodies get
around in all
different ways.

Even babies crawl, but that is just a phase.

Just because some brains work differently, doesn't mean they are dumb.

They can do other great
things, only done by some.

Everybody talks differently,
some talk with their hands.

Some people you just have
to listen more carefully because
they are hard to understand.

Some bodies don't like to talk. That is called being shy. Other bodies are very sensitive and it's easy for them to cry.

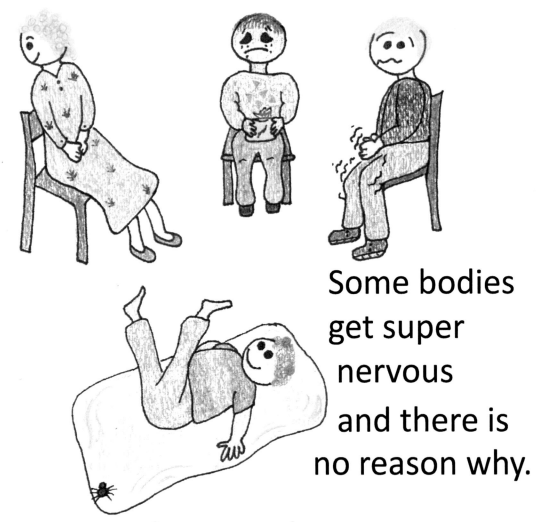

Some bodies get super nervous and there is no reason why.

Some are so hyper and excited, they have so much to say. Others might twitch and wiggle all day.

Some bodies might yell, say weird things, or start running around. That is OK. Their brains just don't want to slow down.

Some might hear or see things that we can't. Others can't remember things or sing a "De-Do" chant.

Some bodies have gotten sick or had accidents happen to make them who they are today.

And other
bodies were
just born that way.

Some have to take medicine
or a pill. No big deal.

But there's one thing that is true

every body has a heart and
feelings just like you!

Some bodies
may be so different
that you might
feel scared inside.

But it would hurt their feelings if
you went somewhere to hide.

Every body likes to have friends and have fun. No body likes to be sad and have none.

So don't look surprised, point, or stare. It really does hurt their feelings in there.

So give them a smile and a
wave "Hi" the next time
you see some body
different go by.

The End......

Did you find the little spider hiding in the pages of the book?
That is Anansi.

Anansi the Spider

A spider considered to be the spirit of all knowledge of stories.

He is also one of the most important characters of West African and Caribbean Folklore. Anansi tales are some of the best-known amongst the Asante people of Ghana. The **Anansi** tales originated from the Ashanti people. Anansi stories were being told in the 1700's AD, because many of the people who were forced to leave Africa and go to America. These stories about Anansi were not written down until about a hundred years ago, so we can't know whether they are the same stories that people told in medieval Africa or not, or how old they really are.

The name "Anansi" is from the Akan language and literally means "spider".

What is different about you or someone you know?

(Draw a picture or place a photo on this page or the next.)

From the Author,

      I decided to write this book for children to help them understand that everyone is different. To help them to not be scared of people's differences and to be understanding. Everyone deserves to be treated with compassion and love. In writing and illustrating this book, I am aware that my illustrations are vague in some aspects. They are meant to be simple for children to relate to. I am in no way meaning to make light of the seriousness of the conditions of others. I feel deeply compassionate about peoples differences. I am sure there are many other issues and conditions that people have that are not listed in the book, and I wish that I could refer to them all. My hope is that we all can care about each other enough to put our differences aside. I believe teaching children compassion and understanding at a young age (or adults at an older age) will make our world a better place. Sincerely,

Karri Andersen

Look for us on the internet

@ www.everybodysdifferentbook.com

and search social media for

Every Body's Different Book.

Please share your pictures, drawings, stories, and more.

We love to see our special people.

Index - referencing to:

Made in the USA
Middletown, DE
12 August 2017